Budget Management for Beginners

Proven Strategies to Revamp Business & Personal Finance Habits. Stop Living Paycheck to Paycheck, Get Out of Debt, and Save Money for Financial Freedom.

Joel Jacobs

Table of Contents

Take Control of Your Future

Money makes the world go around, but it can also leave your stomach turning. The best way to take control of your future is to take control of your finances.

Irrespective of what has happened in your past, you are standing at a crossroads. The decision that lies before you seems quite simple—do I carry on with my current trajectory or do I take the steps now necessary to secure my future financially? The mere fact that you have spent your hard-earned money on this book means that you are on the verge of choosing the latter, but probably not 100% sure yet how to get started. I am not going to lie to you—the journey you are about to embark on will not be easy. You will need to unlearn every single bad habit that you have been carrying with you from your childhood.

It is very likely that the bad money habits you have now were picked up from past generations, and if you don't make the change now, you will pass it on to future generations. From the onset of this book, you should know that the common bad habits you will need to drop include: not having a budget, overspending, running up debt, and spending little bits of money every day on small luxuries.

In order to avoid living paycheck to paycheck, you will need to find a strategy that works for you. Success won't be immediate—it will take time to break the bad habits from the past and to set yourself up for the future. You will need to find a balance between paying for the past, planning for the future, and living in the now.

The objective of this book is to provide you with the basic skills that will empower you to manage your money better. Managing money is actually not complex—you just need to learn how to cover your current expenses, have something set aside for a rainy day, and plan for the future.

When starting out on this new journey, you will need to make decisions about the following aspects related to your finances:

- Cash management
- Investments
- Family protection
- Retirement planning
- Estate planning

During the course of this book, we will briefly look at the first four aspects, but we will not delve into estate planning. (Estate planning is a specialty field and deals with how your assets will be managed once you are dead or if you become incapacitated.) The objective of this book is to provide you with the necessary skills to avoid living from paycheck to paycheck, in order for you to live a life that is filled with breathtaking experiences and is free from anxiety brought about by living on the edge of your financial means.

Step 1—Budget

Initially, it may feel quite overwhelming to create a budget, but it is the first step you need to take in order to set yourself on the path to financial freedom.

No matter how much money you make on a monthly basis, is it *not* beyond your means to pay your debts and start saving money—if you have a well-planned budget, half the battle is already won.

Like most things in life, you will only achieve success if you follow the basic principles of planning, namely:

- Determine the current status of your finances.
- Set a target, set a due date, and determine the path to reach your target.
- Identify milestones along the way that will serve as indicators that you are still on the right path.
- Implement your plan.
- Regularly review your progress.
- Regularly review your plan.

Your budget will be the foundation of the entire process but the reviews will be the plaster that keeps everything together. Things change (life happens), your financial plan and savings targets will not be the same in five years so be willing to make changes along the way.

How to Budget

It is safe to assume that you are probably aware of what your monthly income is, so the first step in developing your budget is to determine how much money you actually spend in any given month. This might mean that you will need to write down every single expense on a daily basis in order to get an accurate picture. Remember to include ad hoc expenses, like annual subscription fees, in your budget in order to avoid potential shortfalls when the time arrives for the expense to be realized.

You will need to capture the data in a sheet—use either Excel or a free template from the internet. For the purpose of this exercise, we will create a fictional scenario. Let's meet Tom.

Tom is a 35-year-old single dad. He earns $8,500 per month and wants to set up a college savings account for his eight-year-old son, but he currently has a monthly budget shortfall of $150. He uses his credit card to cover the additional monthly expenses. Tom's sister is currently living with him, rent-free, as he needs additional help every second Saturday when he goes to work. She makes no financial contribution to the household even though she earns more than Tom on a monthly basis. Below is a list of all Tom's monthly expenses.

- *Rent $2000 (including utilities)*
- *Groceries $2000*
- *Gym membership $150 (he hasn't been to the gym in the past 4 years)*
- *Vehicle upkeep and fuel $450*
- *Cable $150*
- *School-related expenses $350*
- *Credit card bill $50*
- *Phone related expenses $ 150*
- *Clothing $200*
- *Entertainment $350 (this includes going to restaurants and other leisure expenses)*
- *Insurance $350*
- *Student loan $500*
- *Pet-related expenses $150*
- *Bank charges $350*
- *Financial support to his parents $1000*

Tom realized that these were his monthly expenses after carefully tracking everything over the course of one month, and doing a high-level review of the major expenses from previous months.

Once you (and Tom) have made a summary of all anticipated and unanticipated major expenses, the next step will be to evaluate what your long-term financial goals are. Do you want to be debt-free in three years? Buy your own house? Go on a Greek holiday? Retire comfortably?

For Tom, his priorities are to start an emergency fund (the last emergency trip to the veterinarian cost him over $500) and to start saving for his son to go to a good college one day. Tom's sister also advised that he may need to start putting money away towards his retirement if he doesn't want his son to have to take care of him one day—as he now has to help take care of his parents.

In order for Tom to be able to afford all these long-term goals, he will need to find at least $1000 per month extra. He won't be able to generate other sources of income, so he will need to reduce his expenses—but where to begin?

If you are in the same position as Tom and you need to find a way to cut your expenses, the best place would be to start by figuring out which expenses are necessary (mandatory) and which are not (discretionary).

Mandatory expenses, according to Davis (2021) are those expenses that are difficult to avoid such as expenses related to:

- Housing
- Transportation
- Groceries
- Utilities
- Health care
- Child care
- Debt
- Savings

Davis (2021) lists the following as discretionary expenses which more often than not are the budget items where savings can be found:

- Foods and drinks prepared outside the home
- Clothing and accessories
- Cosmetics and personal products

8

- Electronics
- Alcohol and tobacco
- Gifts
- Entertainment
- Travel

Based on the two lists above, it is very likely that Tom may have forgotten some expenses and that he is actually overspending much more frequently than he originally calculated, meaning that his debt burden may be larger than he actually anticipates.

Honesty is the foundation of the budgeting process, and if you are not honest about where your money is going, you are never going to find the source of your spending problems.

It might sound a bit harsh, but in all likelihood, the main factor in your current situation of living from paycheck to paycheck (or even worse from paycheck to debt to paycheck) is spending too much money on discretionary items.

Cutting Expenses / Increasing Your Income

After you have gone through the budgeting process, you may very well realize that you are either spending up to the very last cent of your income, or you may even have reached a point where you are increasing your debt burden by using your credit card as a secondary 'income'. If you are living beyond your income, it is also very likely that you are not building up your savings. If you are in this space, you will need to start cutting back on expenses.

Below are a few tips to consider in order to reduce your monthly expenses:

- Cut back on your energy bill.
- Reduce your grocery bill.
- Prioritize paying off your debt.
- Adjust your cell phone or cable bill to avoid overage fees.

- Avoid trips to restaurants, bars, and coffee shops.
- Plan your trips to the grocery store.
- Avoid expensive hobbies.
- Find free opportunities for exercise and entertainment.
- Pay your debt on time.
- Cancel monthly subscriptions.

Part of the budgeting process also entails that you keep yourself accountable for your expenses. The only way to do this is to capture your daily expenses and track them against the amount you budgeted for them every month. Once you have reached the limit of your budget, then you can no longer have any expenditure in that category.

An easy example—you love sushi and have included $100 per month for sushi in your budget. You get your salary on the 1st of the month, your friend has their birthday on the 5th and you all go out for dinner at your favorite sushi restaurant. By the end of the evening, you are a few drinks strong and declare vehemently that you are paying for everyone—the final bill is $150. Not only have you spent your entire sushi budget at the beginning of the month, you now need to cut spending on another budget line item as well. So for the remainder of the month, you are not allowed to have your favorite treat.

In order to determine whether or not an expense is warranted, ask yourself one simple question—do I want it, or do I need it?

Going back to Tom, his options in terms of cutting expenses are to:

- Cancel his gym membership.
- Calculate how much a babysitter would cost him twice a month compared to his sister living permanently with them (taking into consideration the additional grocery and utility expenses).
- Reduce his entertainment budget.
- Reduce his clothing budget.
- Put a limit on the amount of time his son can spend on the phone.

You might reach a point where you are no longer able to cut your expenses, but you still need to create more cash. Apart from robbing a bank (don't rob a bank), the only other alternatives for generating more cash is to expand your income stream. This can be done by starting a business on the side, by getting a second job, or by selling unnecessary goods.

Step 2—Fight the Debt Trap

Americans owed more than $1 trillion in credit card debt alone, with a significant jump in debt occurring during the holiday season. 75% of individuals who had credit card debt at the start of 2020 indicated that they would not be able to repay those debts before interest would be charged (Epperson & Dickler, 2020).

Debt is a significant hurdle on the road to reaching your financial goals. If you are in debt, you are less likely to be able to build up any discernible savings and you will be forced to decide whether to prioritize debt repayment or saving.

Some of the advantages of prioritizing debt repayment on your journey towards financial freedom include:

- Reducing the overall cost of your debt by reducing the amount of interest paid over time.
- Improving your credit score.
- Enabling you to focus on savings and other financial goals once you are debt-free.
- Removing the emotional burden associated with debt.
- Enabling you to free up money to invest in experiences that you enjoy.
- Avoiding the threat of losing everything when life goes around an unexpected corner because you are able to own your assets.

Why Debt Is More Expensive Than You Think

Debt is sometimes more expensive than we anticipate because we often forget about the interest added to any debt incurred. Let's quickly do a bit of math to better understand the crux of the problem—here is our fictional friend Tom again to create our next scenario:

Tom owes $1,000 on his credit card, with an annual interest rate of 18%
charged on the debt. He has one of two options available to him—Option 1
is paying only the minimum amount payable, which is $50 per month.
Option 2 is to pay $100 per month. How much will his debt cost him at the
end of the day?

It might seem as if Option 1 would be the preferred option because
he will only need to pay $50 every month, but over time his debt will
cost him more than $100 more to repay over a longer period of time.
With the interest rate at 18% per year, it will take Tom two years to
repay the debt, with an additional $197.83 paid in interest. If Tom
chooses Option 2, he will only need eleven months to repay his debt,
with the interest amounting to $91.62 only.

Therefore, by opting to pay off his debt in a shorter period of time,
he ultimately saves $106.20 and is debt-free thirteen months earlier
than if he only opted for the minimum amount payable.

The Devil Is in the Details

When it comes to debt, make sure that you check the details. In other
words—study your bill on a monthly basis, and make sure you
understand the fine print on any debt you incur.

Always check your bill—mistakes can be made or people can
deliberately try to defraud you, so always make sure that you go
through whatever bill you need to pay to ensure that it is the right
amount and includes the cost of only the services rendered. By doing
this, you not only avoid paying for something that you don't have
to pay for, but you also start getting a better understanding of how
your debt is put together—especially the amount of interest you
need to pay or any penalties that might occur if the debt is not
settled in time.

The fine print of a contract is all the important information that is
excluded from the main body of the document and is often included
as either addendums or footnotes. Information that the document

issuer does not want you to pay attention to, but should actually know, is normally hidden in the fine print.

Most people may don't consider reading the fine print as important as reading the instructions. But at least with instructions, you can still retrace your steps, and fish the box from the trash—once you sign any form of loan or credit agreement there is no going back.

Though some of the costs related to the fine print may seem insignificant at first, a lot of small expenses tend to accumulate over time and can be as devastating to your cash flow as single large expenditures.

Here are a few steps you can take in order to protect yourself when it comes to contractual legalese:

- Take time to review the documents and ask questions about clauses that you do not understand.
- Seek the advice of legal experts, especially in instances where you are incurring major debts.
- When buying anything "as is", get a second opinion on the condition of the item you are purchasing before you sign the final documentation, in order to avoid buying yourself a hole in your pocket.

Debt Repayment Strategies

In order to get out of debt, you need to have a strategy as well as a deadline for when you want to be debt-free.

If you have more than one source of debt, one strategy might be to prioritize which debt is settled first. Though you will need to try and make some sort of payment on all the debt you face, it is best to settle debts with higher interest rates or those with penalties attached to them first in order to reduce the overall cost of your debt over time.

Another strategy to consider would be to focus first on repaying smaller debts first, as settling those debts might bring about a sense of accomplishment that will keep you motivated to pay off the remaining debts.

A third option to consider is borrowing money to pay off all other debts, in order to have only one monthly payment. These types of loans are called debt consolidation loans. Before you opt for this strategy make sure that this consolidated loan will still cost you less per month than the gradual repayment of your separate debts.

At the end of the day, however, you will need to find the strategy that works best for you and stick with it.

Whatever strategy you end up choosing, the following tips can come in handy along your debt repayment journey:

- Make a list of all your debt and write down how much it actually costs you every month.
- Reduce living expenses in order to increase the gap between money in and money out, thus freeing up more cash to either save or pay debt.
- Constantly monitor your progress.

Good Debt

Student and mortgage loans have generally been considered "good debt", as in both instances you owe money on something that can help you earn more money over time or improve your life in important ways. However, considering the current global economy, the only good debt is the debt you have already paid off.

Though a student loan provides you with a degree that can potentially increase your earning ability, and a mortgage means that you have invested in an asset, both can go horribly wrong if you do not read the market correctly.

In the current economic conditions, the likelihood that any new entrant into the job market will be guaranteed a gradually increasing income and job security will be very low for at least the next five years. Therefore, if you are heading towards tertiary education in the next two years, you should try to avoid debt as much as possible. In a few years, however, the world will look much more different and the situation could be a lot better. So the point that you should take away from this is to evaluate the current and potential economic markets to determine if you will be able to afford your debt within the foreseeable future.

The same holds true for mortgages—if you borrow more than you can afford, do not fully understand the terms and conditions of your mortgage, or are investing in a property market that is in the midst of a downward spiral, you are likely to lose your family home to foreclosure. When you borrow money to procure your first home, make sure that you understand how much it is that you can borrow (generally not more than 28% of your gross monthly income) and pay attention to what the housing market is doing at that time.

Nearly 10% of Americans can be considered "house poor", meaning they have taken out mortgages on homes they cannot afford and then end up being unable to cover other expenses, optimize savings opportunities, or invest for future endeavors (Brennan, 2020).

When it comes to debt, don't ask what you can do for your debt, ask what your debt can do for you—or in other words, make sure that if you do incur debt it is for something that can actually improve your wealth in the future, but don't incur debt if you will not be able to afford it.

How to Avoid Debt

Debt that should be avoided at all costs is any debt you may incur when purchasing something that loses its value over time, or which is consumed within a short period of time. This includes debts related to vehicles, clothes and consumables, and holidays. Taking out payday loans and using credit cards for these types of purchases means that the final cost of these items can easily be in excess of

200% higher than the initial cost, due to penalties and exorbitant interest rates.

Before you enter into new debt, ask yourself the following questions:

- Does the debt make sense taking into consideration how much you would need to repay?
- Will you be able to recover almost all your money or even more through the purpose of the debt?
- Are there better options available to you to utilize the money that will actually contribute to your future financial security?

Most young Americans have a significant debt burden to deal with once they leave college—due to student loans. In order to avoid starting out far below zero when you enter the job market, try to avoid taking out student loans that will exceed in total what you are likely to earn in your first year being employed.

Other tips which may prove useful in avoiding an increased debt burden while in the process of repaying existing debts include:

- Avoid purchases that you cannot afford without going into debt.
- Cut up your credit card—if you don't have it, you can't use it.
- Pay daily living expenses with cash. A good technique for providing a bit of a spending reality check is to put all funds to be used for living expenses in an envelope and use the envelope for all payments. This way, you can literally see the money flow from your pocket
- Ignore friends and family who are overspending—you can provide them with advice on how to improve their own financial position, but you are not obliged to provide them with financial assistance if it means that you will not be able to pay your dues.
- Say no to unnecessary outings and expenses.
- Pay your debts on time and avoid additional penalties and fees.

Step 3 - Don't Keep up with the Jones's

"Keeping up with the Jones's" is an idiom that stems from the early 1900s and refers to the constant conscious or subconscious comparison you might be making between your lifestyle and those of your peers. This behavior often results in a feeling of inadequacy that could eventually translate into debt if you actively attempt to copy those you measure yourself against. Your story is not their story and it will always be best to live below your means since whoever you are trying to impress will not pay your debts.

Going into debt in order to fund your lifestyle means that your lifestyle is unsustainable in the long run and the true cost of debt goes beyond your bank balance since overspending will have a negative influence on your mental wellbeing.

So before you swipe that credit card on something cool you saw on social media, ask yourself the following questions:

- Why do I want this?
- Do I really need it?
- How long will I use this?
- Can I afford this?

More often than not, the Jones's we are chasing are not even friends and neighbors, but strangers on social media. Their life is not your life; you don't know how much debt they have or whether or not they actually outright own any of the things they put on display (it might all very well be fake). So do yourself a favor and let the Jones's go. These steps will get you off to a good start:

- Focus on yourself and your future and follow the plan that will get you there.
- Live with gratitude.
- Enjoy life within your financial boundaries.
- Check your social media circle—some people may actually have a toxic influence on your mental wellbeing (unfollow them).

Just remember—it is highly unlikely that anybody will post their debt balloon proudly on Instagram.

Maximizing your own social media likes will also have little influence on how those who love you the most will remember you one day. The influencer lifestyle is not sustainable; rushing around, trying to draw the fickle attention of social media scrollers is not a long-term career and the likelihood that you will still have the same following five years from now is very unlikely. Though you might not be actively seeking the influencer lifestyle, you may still secretly be looking for online validation. Do not let the like of likes drag you into a pit of debt. You will not worry about the number of likes you had on a plate of food at a restaurant that you couldn't afford when you are seventy—you will, however, worry about where your next meal will come from if you did not adequately prepare for retirement.

One of the greatest investments you can make is to learn to move away from the "fear of missing out" and start embracing the "joy of missing out".

Focus on keeping up with your goals, rather than chasing the Jones's. Figure out what will be important to you ten years from now, and chase that. Find ways to create your own happiness—you are the only person that can influence how happy you are. Let others find their own path to happiness.

If you want to buy happiness, focus on purchases that will translate into experiences, will be an unexpected treat for yourself or someone else, will make life a bit easier by increasing your free time, will delay gratification, or are an investment in somebody else's success.

Step 4 - Plan for a Rainy Day

You don't know what you don't know, so it is best to plan for the unknown.

Paying off debts is one of the key strategies to execute if you want to ensure future financial stability, but you still need to find a balance between living, paying off debt, and saving money.

Though debt repayment should always be a priority on your journey towards financial freedom, getting into the savings game early also holds some advantages, such as:

- The longer you can save, the more time compound interest has to work its magic.
- Being able to work towards other goals earlier, rather than having to wait for debt to be repaid.
- Avoiding future debt by having an emergency fund available when the unexpected happens.

The debt trap can sneak up on you incrementally or can rush in from left field and tackle you off your feet—that is where planning for a rainy day comes into the picture. Paying off your debt is important but having an emergency fund is just as important, as it is one of the best ways to avoid going into severe debt suddenly.

The idiom "to save money for a rainy day" has been around for well over 500 years and usually refers to setting money aside in order to satisfy a need in the future. Over the past few years GoFundMe campaigns have been used by many as a way to fund emergency expenses, but you cannot rely on the goodness of friends and strangers to dig you out of unforeseen expenses—especially medical expenses—on a regular basis. Eventually, goodwill will run out and you will need to keep your financial boat afloat by yourself.

So before you have to rely on charity to pay major expenses, start setting up an emergency fund for that rainy day.

How Much Is Enough

Financial advisors generally recommend that your emergency fund be substantial enough to cover three to six months' worth of personal expenses. It will take some time to get there, but don't stop putting money into your emergency fund once you have reached your initial target. You will never regret having too much money in your "rainy day" account, but you will always regret not having enough.

If the day does come that you need to dip into your emergency funds, be sure to replace whatever you took out, as you may be faced with another emergency sooner than anticipated.

When setting up your emergency fund, make sure that the money is accessible but not so easily accessible that you are tempted to use it for splurges here and there. The easier it is for you to access your emergency fund, the more likely it is that you might dip into the fund for non-emergency reasons. Try to find a savings option that will ensure access to the funds within at least three days, but that could potentially also earn dividends or accumulate good interest over time. You should also avoid high-risk investments when considering various options for investing, as you do not want to face the possibility of lost investments when you are already facing another emergency.

In some instances, setting up a reasonable nest egg might need to be prioritized over paying off debt, especially in circumstances with a high probability of significant unforeseen expenses, or if job security is not guaranteed.

The final decision between whether you should focus on savings or debt repayment will be based on your own personal financial goals.

Is Insurance Necessary?

Taking out, or having insurance, refers to the process of paying scheduled fees to an insurance company in order to be able to reclaim money from them in the event of harm befalling a person or object. Insurance coverage can be obtained to cover damages related to property and assets, health care, and/or death.

The three most important insurance types currently available on the market include life insurance, health insurance, and liability insurance. It is best to go over the type of insurance and total coverage required with a qualified professional. Spending money on insurance when you are hardly getting by on your current salary may seem unnecessary, but the long-term benefits will outweigh the short-term costs.

Below are a few reasons why having insurance is beneficial:

- It can ensure your family's financial stability in the event of an emergency.
- It brings peace of mind to know that some of the most significant expenses for your family will be covered in the event of an untimely death or incapacitation.
- It can be used as a tax break.
- It can improve the probability of qualifying for a home or business loan.

The younger you are when you buy insurance, the cheaper it will be. Insurance companies use some serious math to calculate your risk profile and younger people tend to have a better risk profile, this is lifestyle dependent, however.

In early 2020, nearly a third of all working Americans had some kind of medical debt. On average, Americans spent in excess of $5,000 per year on out-of-pocket health care, which can include the cost of medical insurance, but also includes costs related to medication and medical supplies (Leonhardt, 2020). Each year many people are left without medical insurance at a time when they need it most. This results in an escalating debt crisis, as many people avoid going for medical treatment, but then end up with even more significant costs later on when the problem has escalated.

If you are currently in a situation where you have little or no medical insurance and rising medical debts, you probably do not even want to have a conversation about any type of insurance—you just want to get out of debt before your debt is sent for collection and you end up becoming part of the growing number of Americans that have been forced into bankruptcy as a result of unpayable medical expenses.

Before you become completely despondent about the medical debt mountain in front of you, just remember that most service providers will be satisfied with having debts settled over a period of time, as opposed to not having the debt settled at all. Therefore, try to negotiate a debt payment plan or seek the advice of a medical billing advocate to help you negotiate your current reality.

Planning for Retirement

Retirement planning is essential to ensure that you can be financially independent and able to respond to whatever life throws at you at a time in your life when your earning potential has shrunk to zero. In your twenties, it may seem like an absolutely ridiculous idea to start planning for retirement, but the younger you are when you start thinking about the day that you are old, the better it will work out for you in the end. When planning for retirement, you will need to anticipate possible living expenses as well as medical expenses.

When you plan for your retirement the financial component is critical, but you should not lose sight of the quality of life component as well. Retirement is the time when you should be able to enjoy all the hard work you have put in, and whether that means being able to take a nap whenever you want or travel the world with your friends, your planning should be done in such a way that you have sufficient resources in order to attain the quality of life you aspire to in retirement.

We have listed below some more reasons as to why retirement planning is important.

- Most countries have a maximum age at which you can no longer seek formal employment.
- People are living longer than before, so retirement funds will need to last longer as well.
- The older you get, the more likely you are to develop medical emergencies.
- Having only one source of income when you retire can be very risky—especially if it is funded by the government.
- Your children cannot be used as your retirement plan.

The process of retirement planning can be described—in a nutshell—as the process of setting income goals for retirement and identifying the actions that will need to be executed in order to achieve those goals. It is generally recommended to plan for having access to between 70% - 90% of your pre-retirement income in order to live a good life.

The best time to start planning for retirement is the moment you start working, but even if you are a few years behind, don't fret. Start planning and investing in your retirement now—better late, than never.

Planning for your retirement is not brain surgery, but you may require professional assistance along the way to provide you with all the information you may need in order to make decisions about:

- The age at which you want to retire.
- Potential future expenses based on current expenses and potential future changes in circumstances.
- The best portfolio mix that takes into consideration your goals.
- The best options to make up for lost time.

Living within your means and saving money can often seem like a tedious task, so one of the easiest ways to trick yourself into saving money is to ensure that whatever you are planning on saving is already out of your account and into your investment before you even realize it is gone.

Some employers have savings programs at work—talk to the relevant persons within your workplace and find out whether or not your company has such a program and whether or not you qualify for it. Just make sure you read the fine print and that the savings program aligns with your needs. Try to maximize the amount of money you can invest in such a program, especially if there is the option of the employer matching whatever the employee contributes up to a maximum amount.

If you create a retirement fund outside your work environment, avoid using the money you have set aside for retirement for other purposes. The money must be left undisturbed for as long as possible in order to maximize the benefits of compound interest.

The Beauty of Compound Interest

Compound interest is the interest you receive on not only the original capital invested, but also on the interest that you have accumulated throughout the duration of your savings. Basically, it is interest on interest (Fernando, 2019). With any investment or savings you are likely to generate interest, but compound interest will ensure that your invested amount will grow faster than simple interest.

When you are investing money, always look for compound interest; when you are taking out a loan, always try to avoid compound interest.

Let's talk about Tom again.

Tom repaid his debt in eleven months and opted to create a savings fund for his son (who is currently eight years old) with the $91.62 that he *originally saved on his credit card debt. He is planning on saving for ten years at a fixed interest rate of 5%, with an additional monthly payment of $50 to the investment. With compound interest added on an annual basis, Tom's son will have $7,695.97 in his savings fund by the time he turns eighteen years old. Tom contributed $6,091.62, while earning $ 1,604.3 in interest. If Tom's son continues saving at the same rate as his father until he is forty years old, he would have a savings fund of $45,615.86, of which $19,291.62 was contributed by Tom and his father, and $26,324.24 was earned through compound interest.*

In order to experience the full benefit of earning any form of interest on your savings or investments, you will need to remain patient. Interest accumulates over time, and the more time you have available to wait, the bigger the return will be. That is why it is of critical importance to start saving as soon as possible—especially if you want to be prepared for a rainy day.

Step 5 – Speak to an Expert

"A good plan violently executed now is better than a perfect plan next week,"

- General George S Patton

Though it seems a bit brutal to look at inspiration from a World War II General when it comes to financial planning, General Patton understood the risks of getting stuck in your own mind and "analysis paralysis". Often when we need to make difficult decisions about our own lives, we get overwhelmed with all the information that we need to sort and analyze and never get to a point where we can make a decision and execute it effectively.

Figuring out the best plan for yourself and your family can be daunting, especially if you are under a significant debt burden. Finding the light at the end of the tunnel can seem like a nearly impossible event, and the mounting pressures can start to create significant anxiety. If you ever find yourself in such a situation, it is best to find a qualified expert to offer guidance regarding which options are available to you.

A qualified financial advisor can help you to evaluate your financial needs and can assist with a variety of aspects related to the financial realm—like advice on investments or clarification of tax laws.

Before you engage with any person that claims to be an advisor, ensure that they are registered with the relevant authorities in your area. Do your research before you trust.

Below is a list of potential experts that you can seek guidance from:

- Brokers: Brokers will suggest a selection of investment or insurance products that they deem valuable for you based on your specific goals. These individuals may not necessarily be bound to a fiduciary standard and may at times oversell you on what you need.
- Independent/fee-only advisors: Advisors offer a broader service, so they will be able to provide insight into almost

all aspects of personal financial management such as budgeting, estate planning, debt repayment, and much more. They may either be linked to a broker and be paid commission for products they sell (Independent advisor) or work as a fee-only advisor, obtaining payment from the investments they recommend.

- Planners: Financial planners are the ones you need to engage with when it comes to figuring out how you can turn a little money into a lot, over time. They help you set up a financial plan that will work for you and your family based on your current and potential future needs.
- Money coaches: If you are unsure of what your goals should be, a money coach might be the answer to your problems. They help you see the big picture and can suss out what your objectives are even before you are able to articulate them.
- Debt counselors: In the event that your debt has reached uncontrollable levels, debt counselors may just be the answer to your prayers. They can help you set up a plan that will work for you—that allows you to still have a semblance of a life—while still paying off your debts. They may even be able to negotiate a repayment plan with lower interest rates and reduced penalties.
- Investment advisors: These individuals can only provide advice on an investment strategy as well as the potential investments to consider. Make sure that you choose an advisor that is not under obligation to sell a certain amount of investments on a monthly basis.
- Accountants: Accountants are often the butt of jokes in the media, but they play a vital role in ensuring that you remain solvent and on the right side of tax services.

Never feel ashamed to ask for help. Not everybody can be an expert in everything and, though Google is an awesome tool, you may still need to consult with a trained professional in order to figure out the final details of what you need and how you are going to get there. Just remember—expert advice will not come cheaply but in the end, it can be a great investment for your own future. Make sure that you can afford the expense of going to an advisor because it is of little value to engage with a financial management expert if the whole process of consultation is beyond your financial means.

Knowing when to engage with an expert is half the battle, but the general consensus is that you should seek expert advice under the following circumstances: you are within five years of retiring, you have reached a milestone like buying a house or being accepted to university, or your income has suddenly increased.

When looking for somebody to assist you in setting up a long-term plan for you and your family, do your research—don't go to the first person recommended by an acquaintance of an acquaintance. Try to avoid individuals that work on a commission basis only, and remember, if it is too good to be true, it is probably a scam. Unfortunately, when it comes to proper financial management and planning, slow and steady is the only sustainable approach to follow.

Though there is no law that prevents it, it tends to be best not to turn to your friends or family even though they may be qualified financial advisors. You will need to take emotion out of the process which will not always be easy when you are too familiar with your advisor. You will need somebody that can be objective and strict during the planning process and a friend or family member might try to spare your feelings, while you will not have that luxury with a stranger.

It can, however, be daunting to rely on the advice of a complete stranger when it comes to your future, so do some research about whether or not financial advisors need to be registered with an external body in your country. Though it is not a guarantee that you will not be scammed, there is at least still some comfort in the fact that the person helping you plan for your future can be held accountable by a legal entity.

Once you have had a conversation with your advisor, remember one thing—it is still your money. You don't have to feel bad if you want a second opinion. Don't be forced into making a decision that you are not yet comfortable with or sign contracts if you are not sure of the hidden costs and commissions involved. You have the right to ask questions—whether you earn $1,000 per month or $100,000.

Initially, you may feel a bit underprepared to have a meeting with an advisor, since you may not understand a lot of the complexities of financial markets and financial management. There is, however, a simple hack for overcoming this barrier—follow the right people online.

Like we previously said—don't just trust one opinion, as there will never be just one resource that will cover the complexities of your personal experience. Diversify your sources of information and listen to different points of view.

Providing a comprehensive list of individuals to learn from on social media platforms would be near impossible, but try to avoid anybody that sells themself as an "influencer". A timeless approach to getting a quick list to sort through would be to ask your preferred search engine for a list of financial experts to follow online.

Though these online experts will not replace the value of talking to an advisor, engaging with them from afar will help broaden your personal knowledge base and put you on the path to greater understanding.

Technology can also be a valuable tool to track your spending or savings. There are a great number of apps currently available that can help you track your daily spending, adherence to your budget, and progress towards your savings goals.

It may seem to be a bit excessive to track your daily spending or to check in on the progress towards your savings goals on a regular basis, but it can also serve as a needed reality check and a silent accountability partner on this new journey towards financial freedom.

Step 6 - Save Now, Spend Later

Under most circumstances, people will have a savings account for one of three reasons:

- To have sufficient money in case of an emergency.
- To reduce the amount of money needed when applying for a loan.
- To have a bit of fun by spoiling themselves with something a bit extravagant.

We have already covered saving for a rainy day, so now we will spend some time on the other two reasons—taking money from yourself today so your future self can have some fun later and putting away savings in order to reduce your debt burden when you do need a loan in future. It is especially important to know how long you have to invest, as that will also have an influence on the type of investments you would consider.

While having an emergency fund and a retirement fund is great, you actually want to live life in the here and now as well. It is good to have long-term savings, but you can also set up a "splash" fund for things such as holidays or new electronics—anything that gives you joy outside the everyday drudgery. Such items will normally be part of your short-term savings plan that should cover larger planned expenses that will occur within the next two years.

You can even start building savings for bigger ticket items such as a home or a new car. Though you may not be able to save enough to buy either of these two without debt, it can make debt a lot smaller if you start saving now to at least reduce the size of the loan. These items are normally incorporated into your medium-term savings and should cover planned expenses that are likely to occur within the next five to 10 years.

Whether or not you are establishing a short or medium-term saving, the principles will remain the same —have a budget and have a plan.

Once you have settled your debts and have built up a bit of savings, you can let your hair hang loose by including line items in your budget for monthly treats, like a trip to your favorite fancy restaurant or a few new books.

Avoiding impulse buys

The one habit you need to break to ensure that you can maintain the momentum that you have built up is impulse buying.

Impulse buying is often triggered by emotions and results in the purchase of goods and services without planning the purchase in advance. This behavior can either be triggered by anxiety and unhappiness or can result in anxiety and unhappiness; therefore, reduced psychological well-being can either be a cause of financial problems or can be created by them.

Impulse buyers frequently share some characteristics, such as:

- Being status-conscious and image-concerned, and therefore like to look good in the eyes of others.
- Having high levels of anxiety and difficulty controlling emotions.
- Having low happiness levels and looking towards shopping for a short-term high brought about by the spending spree endorphin rush.
- Not thinking about the long-term consequences of their actions—just looking for the instant gratification offered by impulse buying.

According to Cruze (2020), the average American spends over $5000 annually on impulse buys. This translates to just over $400 per month and if this monthly expenditure was put into a savings account (even at minimal interest rates) it would be worth over $25,000 after only five years. You are therefore losing a significant potential investment opportunity—all thanks to unhealthy emotions.

In order to break the habit of impulse buying, make the following behaviors part of your daily habits:

- Stick to your budget.
- Allow yourself some opportunity to spend—just make sure this line item on your budget is reasonable and affordable.
- Take time and think about the purchase before you act.
- Don't go shopping without a plan.
- Don't add yourself to email lists.
- Avoid shopping when you are emotional.
- Don't shop alone.
- Leave your credit card at home.
- Stop comparing yourself to others.
- Challenge your friends to a no-spend challenge.
- Keep your goals in mind.

If you have thought about an item for a while and realize that it is something you absolutely cannot go without, create a short-term savings plan for the item by adjusting your budget in order to be able to afford it a few months down the line—with the added benefit of NO additional debt.

How to Maintain Momentum

Living within your means might be a novelty at the beginning, but after a few months of restricting yourself, you might be tempted to chuck the plan in the nearest river and go and buy yourself something nice. In order to maintain momentum, you have to make budgeting a habit, and a habit will take time. You might even need to change your thinking about money and budgets—in the end budgeting does not limit your freedom, it actually gives you the wings to fly. Once you start believing it, half the battle is won.

Changing the way you think about money will not happen overnight and you might need to do a bit of work to make the change. Below are a few tips that may help you change your money mindset:

- Read more books that will have a positive impact on your thinking.
- Be generous.
- Have a picture in mind for your retirement.
- Believe that you will achieve.

Initially, the only way to maintain momentum when it comes to this new journey of financial freedom is to take emotion and willpower out of the equation. If you have to decide on a monthly basis whether or not you are going to send $100 to a savings account, you will opt to do something fun with the money, instead of saving it.

Setting up automatic transfers means that you take the thinking out of the process, and you get used to the money just not being available anymore after a while. In this way, you ensure that saving can happen in an effortless and consistent manner.

It is also important to set goals for yourself. Goals provide you with a destination and it is easier to maintain momentum if you know what the destination is, and by when you would like to reach it.

Something else that you will need to focus on is to be present in your own life. By being more self-aware you will be able to start identifying potential triggers for the emotions that could result in an expensive shopping spree. By being able to read situations or emotions that could derail your savings train, you can learn to regulate yourself and thus potentially avoid significant, unplanned expenses.

Never lose sight of the big picture. While it is important to focus on the small victories, your destination is what will ultimately serve as the biggest motivator to not go off track. There was a reason why you decided that living from one paycheck to the next is not the final reality that you want to settle for. Never forget that "why".

Step 7 - Living generously

"What good shall I do this day?" - Benjamin Franklin

According to Livingston (n.d), happiness economists have found that giving money to help others is often one of the most rewarding ways to spend money.

Regardless of your current financial situation, try to start including a category for donations into your budget. By planning to live generously, you make it a priority instead of an afterthought. By giving, even if you think you can't afford it, you start to live outwards and move beyond selfishness while gradually becoming more aware of the needs of others. The discipline needed to accommodate even the smallest generosity when you are trying to get and stay out of debt can also serve you well in the overall practice of being responsible with your money.

You might be asking the question to yourself now—why must I be generous if I have to cut down on Starbucks or take out or other things that make me happy? Giving with an open heart and mind provides benefits beyond the instant gratification of a soy latte.

Below are some of the benefits that you may experience once you start living a more generous life:

- People who live generously have been found to have greater satisfaction with life and appear to be happier all around.
- Relationships tend to be stronger and more reciprocal in those that are considered to be generous.
- People who tend to give more easily are happier in their careers.
- Generous individuals tend to have a more positive outlook on life.
- Due to higher satisfaction levels and a more positive disposition, mental and physical health tend to be higher in those that are more generous.
- Once you start looking outwards—seeing the need of others—you become more satisfied with what you have

and tend to care a lot less about "keeping up with the Jones's".

- Generous people tend to have higher self-esteem and this can be a great counter to the need for indulging in retail therapy in order to feel better about oneself.
- Generous people are often willing to work harder and will do what it takes to achieve their goals since they see their own success as not only being of benefit to them but also to others.

One of the greatest investments you can make in your future self is to learn to be more generous. Even if you cannot spare a single cent initially, you can still be generous with your time or other resources, without it costing you anything. Regardless of how you decide to live more generously, doing so will definitely change your life for the better. Once you realize that others' success will not diminish your own, a ripple effect can be created that uplifts entire communities and, the more successful those around you become, the more successful you actually become.

Generosity does have a dark side as well, especially when you give with the expectation of receiving something in return or if you have people that might look at exploiting your generosity for their own benefit. You should always give without expectation and trust that others are honest in their motivations, but remain aware of the pitfalls and re-evaluate the situation when you realize that you may be sucked into the dark side of generosity. Learn to say no without feeling bad about it.

Thinking should be part of the process of being generous. Don't force your generosity onto somebody or give because it is on your to-do list for the day. True generosity comes from a place where you have identified a need in others, and realize that you have something that could be of benefit to them.

Keep up the Good Work

The road to financial freedom will be paved with patience and declined take-out. There are no quick fixes and the only option will be to concentrate on your plan—one step at a time. Always keep an eye on how far you have come, celebrate when you reach a milestone, and keep at it.

Life would have been so much easier if we had learned more about personal financial management when we were a lot younger. One of the best investments you can make in your own future financial well-being is to ensure that your children learn financial management skills from a young age. The best way they will learn about money is by watching how you work with money, but it is important to ensure that they understand why you do things in a certain way. That understanding will only be fostered by having conversations with them and exposing them to the basic principles of budgeting at a young age.

The younger they are when they start saving, the better. The beauty of compound interest is that, even if they start saving just $10 per month at the age of eight, they will have a nice little nest egg by the time they leave school. Many parents compromise their own financial future when they have to bail out their children when their financial planning fails them; teach them young and they might not need you or your emergency fund as their emergency fund when they are older.

The basic principles for setting yourself up for financial freedom to be instilled in all children and adults are as follows:

- Have a budget.
- Stick to your budget.
- Pay your debt.
- Start building a reserve for emergencies.

Once your financial situation starts improving, you will be tempted to increase your expenditure as well. The improvement might be because you are starting to see the benefits of financial planning or might be a result of an increase in income. Whatever the reason for the extra money left over at the end of the month, try to resist the urge to splurge. Rather, increase your savings—either towards your emergency fund or towards an item that you have long dreamed about. Try to avoid splashing cash on items that will only result in instant gratification, but not in long-term satisfaction.

At the end of the day, you want your money to work for you—don't get stuck in a cycle of squirreling money away in a savings account. Yes, it is good to have money in an emergency fund, but once you become more financially mobile, start diversifying your investments in order to ensure that you have diversified exposure to risks and opportunities—the ideal is to have your money earn money without you having to do much about it.

The last thought I would like to leave you with is this—remember to give, but don't give beyond what you can afford. Society was built on the premise of people helping each other when they were in a position to do so, so try to live more generously—not only for the benefit of others but also for yourself.

If you enjoyed this book in anyway, an honest review is always appreciated!

References

5 Budgeting Basics to Create a Budget That Works | Discover. (2017, August 22). Discover Bank - Banking Topics Blog. https://www.discover.com/online-banking/banking-topics/5-budgeting-basics/

5.1 The Budget Process | Personal Finance. (n.d.). Courses.lumenlearning.com. https://courses.lumenlearning.com/suny-personalfinance/chapter/5-1-the-budget-process/

9 Reasons Why Retirement Planning Is Important | Pure Financial Advisors, Inc. (2018, April 6). Pure Financial Advisors, Inc. https://purefinancial.com/learning-center/blog/why-retirement-planning-is-important/

11 quotes that show the great leadership of General George Patton. (2015, December 21). Business Insider. https://www.businessinsider.com/11-quotes-that-show-the-great-leadership-of-general-george-patton-2015-11#2-a-good-plan-violently-executed-now-is-better-than-a-perfect-plan-next-week-2

25 Reasons Keeping Up With the Joneses' is a Terrible Pursuit. (2020, April 6). Home Stratosphere. https://www.homestratosphere.com/reasons-keeping-up-with-the-joneses-is-a-terrible-pursuit/

Adcock, S. (2019, May 16). *Keeping up with the Joneses? Don't - most of them are flat broke*. Think Save Retire. https://thinksaveretire.com/the-joneses-are-broke/

AES Financial Services. (n.d.). *Financial Planning Guide - Expert guidance for your financial planning*. Www.aesinternational.com. https://www.aesinternational.com/financial-planning-guide

Alvarez, J. (2020, July 20). *Good debt vs. bad debt: Why what you've been told is probably wrong*. CNBC. https://www.cnbc.com/2020/07/20/good-debt-vs-bad-debt-why-what-youve-been-told-is-probably-wrong.html#:~:text=%E2%80%9CGood%E2%80%9D%20debt%20is%20defined%20as

Becker, J. (n.d.). *9 Ways Generous People See the World Differently*. Becoming Minimalist. https://www.becomingminimalist.com/more-generosity/

Beers, B. (2021, February 19). *Should I Pay off Debt or Invest Extra Cash?* Investopedia. https://www.investopedia.com/articles/pf/08/invest-reduce-debt.asp

Birken, E. G. (2020, March 5). *How To Budget In 7 Simple Steps*. Forbes Advisor. https://www.forbes.com/advisor/personal-finance/how-to-budget-simple-steps/

Borad, S. B. (2020, October 5). *Budgeting Process – Steps and Importance of Budget*. EFinanceManagement. https://efinancemanagement.com/budgeting/budgeting-process#:~:text=The%20budgeting%20process%20is%20the

Brennan, C. (2019, January 28). *Good Debt Vs. Bad Debt*. Forbes Advisor. https://www.forbes.com/advisor/loans/good-debt-vs-bad-debt/

Central Bank. (n.d.). *10 Strategies to Avoid Getting into Debt | Central Bank*. Www.centralbank.net. https://www.centralbank.net/learning-center/strategies-to-avoid-debt/

Chen, J. (2021, February 23). *Learn About Compounding*. Investopedia. https://www.investopedia.com/terms/c/compounding.asp

Compound Interest Calculator | Investor.gov. (n.d.). Www.investor.gov. https://www.investor.gov/financial-tools-calculators/calculators/compound-interest-calculator

Creating a Budget with a Personal Budget Spreadsheet. (2019). Better Money Habits. https://bettermoneyhabits.bankofamerica.com/en/saving-budgeting/creating-a-budget

Cruze, R. (2020a, September 25). *Impulse Buying: Why We Do It and How to Stop*. Daveramsey.com. https://www.daveramsey.com/blog/stop-impulse-buys#:~:text=We%20impulse%20buy%20because%20of

Cruze, R. (2020b, October 21). *How to Change Your Money Mindset*. Daveramsey.com. https://www.daveramsey.com/blog/understanding-your-money-mindset

Daly, L. (2019, November 24). *The 8 Biggest Benefits of Being Generous*. The Ascent. https://www.fool.com/the-ascent/banks/articles/8-biggest-benefits-being-generous/

Davis, G. B. (2021, March 1). *How to make a budget - 5 Steps to get started*. Money Crashers. https://www.moneycrashers.com/how-to-make-a-budget/

English rainy-day phrases explained by Susie Dent. (2018, September 21). *BBC News*. https://www.bbc.com/news/uk-england-42719824

Epperson, S., & Dickler, J. (2020, January 27). *The secret to financial success: Paying off debt*. CNBC. https://www.cnbc.com/2020/01/27/how-to-pay-off-debt.html

Evans, J. (2020, September 10). *Should I Pay Off Debt or Save Money?* Credit Counselling Society. https://nomoredebts.org/blog/dealing-with-debt/should-i-pay-off-debt-or-save-money#:~:text=Paying%20Off%20Debt%20Can%20Improve%20Your%20Credit%20Score&text=However%2C%20by%20paying%20down%20your

Farrington, R. (2018, January 29). *What Type Of Financial Expert Should You Hire For You?* The College Investor. https://thecollegeinvestor.com/21262/type-financial-expert-hire-situation/

Fernando, J. (2019). *Compound Interest Definition*. Investopedia. https://www.investopedia.com/terms/c/compoundinterest.asp

Fine Print: Should you read it or skip it? (n.d.). Www.araglegal.com. https://www.araglegal.com/individuals/learning-center/topics/budget-and-finance/when-fine-print-must-read

Five simple tips help you avoid impulse buying - The Chin Family. (n.d.). Www.ifec.org.hk. https://www.ifec.org.hk/web/en/young-adults/money-management/five-simple-tips-help-you-avoid-impulse-buying.page

Fonville, M. (2020, February 2). *9 Reasons Why Retirement Planning is Important.* Covenant. https://www.covenantwealthadvisors.com/post/9-reasons-why-retirement-planning-is-important

Gailey, A. (2020, July 7). *10 Money Experts You Should Be Following Right Now.* Time. https://time.com/nextadvisor/banking/personal-finance-experts-to-follow/

Generosity | SkillsYouNeed. (n.d.). Www.skillsyouneed.com. https://www.skillsyouneed.com/ps/generosity.html

George, D. (2020, May 11). *3 Reasons Why You Should Read the Small Print.* The Motley Fool. https://www.fool.com/the-ascent/banks/articles/reasons-why-you-should-read-small-print/

Government of Canada, F. C. A. of C. (2012, May 11). *Credit Card Payment Calculator.* Itools-Ioutils.fcac-Acfc.gc.ca. https://itools-ioutils.fcac-acfc.gc.ca/CCPC-CPCC/CCPCCalc-CPCCCalc-eng.aspx

Hall, L. (2018, August 8). *Keeping up with the Joneses is bad for your finances.* Www.morningstar.com.au. https://www.morningstar.com.au/learn/article/keeping-up-with-the-joneses-is-bad-for-your-f/169437#:~:text=Trying%20to%20%22keep%20up%20with

Hedreen, S. (2020, December 28). *How to Read the Fine Print of a Loan Agreement.* Business.com. https://www.business.com/articles/do-understand-the-fine-print-of-your-loan-agreement/

Hickey, J. P. (2015, July 3). *7 Reasons why generous people are successful.* Lifehack. https://www.lifehack.org/289468/7-reasons-generous-people-are-more-likely-successful

Hund, L. (2020, December 7). *Should You Pay Debt Before Saving?* Bankrate. https://www.bankrate.com/banking/savings/these-guidelines-will-help-you-decide-whether-to-pay-down-debt-or-save/

Irby, L. (2020a, February 4). *10 Strategies for Paying Off Your Debt When You're Broke.* The Balance. https://www.thebalance.com/how-to-pay-off-debt-when-you-re-broke-3875583

Irby, L. (2020b, October 31). *9 Reasons to Pay Off Your Debt.* The Balance. https://www.thebalance.com/reasons-to-pay-off-debt-960047

Is Keeping Up With The Joneses Keeping You Broke? (2019, September 1). The Investors Way. https://theinvestorsway.com.au/keeping-up-with-the-joneses/

Keeping Up With The Joneses: The Bad Habit That Costs You. (2020, March 15). Invested Wallet. https://investedwallet.com/keeping-up-with-the-joneses/

Keinath, S. (2018, December 26). *Understanding the basics of a budget.* 4-H Youth Money Management. https://www.canr.msu.edu/news/understanding-the-basics-of-a-budget

Kenton, W. (2020, December 30). *Fine Print.* Investopedia. https://www.investopedia.com/terms/f/fineprint.asp

Kline, B. (2017, May 17). *The Truth About Keeping up with the Joneses.* Thesavvycouple.com. https://thesavvycouple.com/truth-keeping-up-with-the-joneses/

Lee, D. (2016, January 10). *The Psychological Perks of Paying off Debt.* Bankrate.com. https://www.foxbusiness.com/features/the-psychological-perks-of-paying-off-debt

Leonhardt, M. (2020, February 13). *32% of American workers have medical debt—and over half have defaulted on it.* CNBC. https://www.cnbc.com/2020/02/13/one-third-of-american-workers-have-medical-debt-and-most-default.html

Livingston, A. (n.d.). *17 Reasons Why You Should Get Out of Debt - Benefits of Being Debt-Free.* https://www.moneycrashers.com/reasons-get-out-debt/

Luenendonk, M. (2018, February 20). *Budgeting Process: Complete Guide.* Cleverism. https://www.cleverism.com/budgeting-process-complete-guide/

Lusinski, N. (2018, August 26). *11 financial experts share the best money advice they've ever received.* Business Insider. https://www.businessinsider.com/financial-experts-best-money-advice-2018-8

McMaken, L. (2019). *4 Types Of Insurance Everyone Needs.* Investopedia. https://www.investopedia.com/financial-edge/0212/4-types-of-insurance-everyone-needs.aspx

Menton, J. (2020, September 18). *"This IS Going to Bankrupt me": Americans Rack up $45B Worth of Medical Debt in Collections.* USA TODAY. https://www.usatoday.com/story/money/2020/09/18/unemployment-americans-face-45-b-worth-medical-debt-collections/3480192001/

O'Shea, B., & Schwahn, L. (2021, January 13). *Budgeting 101: How to Budget Money.* NerdWallet. https://www.nerdwallet.com/article/finance/how-to-budget

Rainy Day Fund or Emergency Fund. (2017, March 1). QuickBooks Canada. https://quickbooks.intuit.com/ca/resources/cash-flow/rainy-day-fund-emergency-fund/

Ramsey, D. (2018). *Tithes and Offerings.* Daveramsey.com. https://www.daveramsey.com/blog/daves-advice-on-tithing-and-giving

Ramsey, D. (2021, February 23). *25 Ways to Get Out of Debt.* Daveramsey.com. https://www.daveramsey.com/blog/ways-to-get-out-of-debt

Retirement Planning - Importance of Retirement Planning | ICICI Prulife. (n.d.). Www.iciciprulife.com. https://www.iciciprulife.com/retirement-pension-plans/retirement-planning.html

Rieck, D. (2010, March 3). *Give and Grow Rich: The Power of Focused Generosity.* Copyblogger. https://copyblogger.com/give-and-grow-rich/

Rogin, E. (2019, June 17). *Can Generosity Make You Wealthier?* https://www.ellenrogin.com/generosity-benefits-health-wealth-happiness/

Save for a Rainy Day. (n.d.). https://foh.psc.gov/whatwedo/eap/S-F30E-FOH%20Financial%20Future%20Source.pdf

Save something for a rainy day Idiom Definition – Grammarist. (n.d.). Grammarist.com. Retrieved March 8, 2021, from https://grammarist.com/idiom/save-something-for-a-rainy-day/#:~:text=To%20save%20something%20for%20a%20rainy%20day%20means%20to%20set

Scotia Bank. (n.d.). *Importance of Planning for Retirement*. Www.scotiabank.com. https://www.scotiabank.com/ca/en/personal/investing/investing-basics/importance-of-planning-retirement.html#:~:text=Personal%20planning%20is%20important%20because

Shinn, L. (2021, January 25). *Rule of Thumb: Should I Pay Off Debt or Invest for Retirement?* The Balance. https://www.thebalance.com/should-you-pay-off-your-debt-or-invest-356371

Should I Pay Down Debt or Focus on Savings? | Equifax. (n.d.). Www.equifax.com. Retrieved March 8, 2021, from https://www.equifax.com/personal/education/covid-19/debt-repayment-vs-saving-money/

Should you save, or pay off loans and cards? (n.d.). Www.moneyadviceservice.org.uk. Retrieved March 8, 2021, from https://www.moneyadviceservice.org.uk/en/articles/should-i-save-or-pay-off-debt

Sivens, N. S. (2020, March 16). *The 8 Types Of Financial Experts And How They Can Help You*. Girlboss. https://www.girlboss.com/read/financial-advisors

Six Tips on How to Avoid Debt | New York Life. (n.d.). Www.newyorklife.com. https://www.newyorklife.com/articles/avoid-being-young-and-in-debt

Smith, L. (2019). *Good Debt vs. Bad Debt: What's the Difference?* Investopedia. https://www.investopedia.com/articles/pf/12/good-debt-bad-debt.asp

Staff, I. (2020, December 29). *Saving vs. Paying off Debt*. Investopedia. https://www.investopedia.com/financial-edge/0212/saving-vs.-paying-off-debt.aspx

The Australian Parenting Website. (n.d.). *Managing money and avoiding debt*. Raising Children Network.

https://raisingchildren.net.au/grown-ups/family-life/managing-money/money-debt

Three reasons why you should pay off debt and invest at the same time. | *New York Life*. (n.d.). Www.newyorklife.com. https://www.newyorklife.com/articles/3-reasons-why-pay-off-debt-and-invest-at-the-same-time

Vessella, V. (n.d.). *There's Some Cool Psychology Behind Impulse Buys [Infographic]*. Www.repsly.com. https://www.repsly.com/blog/consumer-goods/theres-some-cool-psychology-behind-impulse-buys-infographic

Vohwinkle, J. (2019). *Your 6-Step Guide to Making a Personal Budget*. The Balance. https://www.thebalance.com/how-to-make-a-budget-1289587

Vohwinkle, J. (2020, May 17). *Why Do I Need Insurance?* The Balance. https://www.thebalance.com/insurance-basics-why-do-i-need-insurance-1289684#:~:text=You%20need%20insurance%20to%20protect

What is Budgeting and Why is it Important? | *My Money Coach*. (2000). Mymoneycoach.ca. https://www.mymoneycoach.ca/budgeting/what-is-a-budget-planning-forecasting

What is Impulsive Buying? Definition of Impulsive Buying, Impulsive Buying Meaning - The Economic Times. (2019). The Economic Times. https://economictimes.indiatimes.com/definition/impulsive-buying

What Is Insurance And Why Is It So Important? (2020, June 26). Www.etmoney.com. https://www.etmoney.com/blog/know-everything-about-insurance-and-why-you-should-have-insurance/

What is retirement planning? Why is it important? (2020, September 8). Scripbox. https://scripbox.com/mf/retirement-planning/

What Psychology Knows about Impulse Buying in 2020. (n.d.). Www.newneuromarketing.com. https://www.newneuromarketing.com/what-psychology-knows-about-impulse-buying-in-2020

Why do I need insurance? (n.d.). Great Eastern, Brunei.
https://www.greateasternlife.com/bn/en/personal-
insurance/understand-insurance/why-do-i-need-insurance.html

Why do you need insurance? (2019). Cooperators.ca.
https://www.cooperators.ca/en/Resources/protect-what-
matters/why-do-you-need-insurance.aspx

Yeager, J. (n.d.). *12 Ways to Avoid Impulse Buying and Save Money -
Buyers Remorse, Shopping.* AARP.
https://www.aarp.org/money/budgeting-saving/info-10-
2010/savings_challenge_tips_for_impulse_shopping.html

Zimmerman, I. (2012). *What Motivates Impulse Buying?* Psychology
Today.
https://www.psychologytoday.com/us/blog/sold/201207/what-
motivates-impulse-buying